W9-BOA-666

Volcanoes
of the
World

Author: Sonia Goldie
Graphic Design and Illustrations: Pascalle Estellon and Anne Weiss
Additional Illustrations: Marianne Maury
Translated from the French by Ezra Post

Library of Congress Cataloging-in-Publication Data

Goldie, Sonia.
  [Volcans du monde English]
  Volcanoes of the world / by Sonia Goldie ; illustrated by
Pascalle Estellon and Anne Weiss. — 1st ed.
    p. cm. — (My favorite nature book)
  Includes index.
  ISBN 1-57990-921-3 (hardcover)
  1. Volcanoes—Juvenile literature. 2. Volcanism—Juvenile
literature. I.
Estellon, Pascale, ill. II. Weiss, Anne, ill. III. Title.
  QE522.G65 2007
  551.21—dc22
                2006033504

10 9 8 7 6 5 4 3 2 1

First Edition

Published by Lark Books, A Division of
Sterling Publishing Co., Inc., 387 Park Avenue
South, New York, N.Y. 10016
Original Title: Volcans du Monde
Originally Published by Mila Editions — France
© 1998, Mila Editions

English translation © 2007, Lark Books

Distributed in Canada by Sterling Publishing, c/o Canadian
Manda Group, 165 Dufferin Street, Toronto, Ontario,
Canada M6K 3H6
Distributed in the United Kingdom by GMC Distribution
Services, Castle Place, 166 High Street, Lewes, East Sussex,
England BN7 1XU
Distributed in Australia by Capricorn Link (Australia) Pty
Ltd., P.O. Box 704, Windsor, NSW 2756 Australia
Manufactured in China
All rights reserved

ISBN 13: 978-1-57990-921-5
ISBN 10: 1-57990-921-3
For information about custom editions, special sales,
premium and corporate purchases, please contact Sterling
Special Sales Department at 800-805-5489 or
specialsales@sterlingpub.com.

Discover the Secrets of the Earth

With a rumble, red-hot rock erupts from deep inside the Earth.
A molten mountain rises from the ground. It's an unstoppable, explosive volcano!

Although volcanoes can cause a lot of destruction, they actually perform a very important job. When pressure and gases build up inside the Earth, they need to go somewhere. Volcanic eruptions let the pressure and gases escape. People have always been fascinated by the power of volcanoes. The Romans believed the god Vulcan lived in a volcano where he made weapons, sending up clouds of smoke and ash. Ancient Hawaiians thought volcanoes erupted when the goddess Pele was angry. She made the Hawaiian Islands while fighting with her sister. Today people are still fascinated by how volcanoes work.

Water and

In the beginning, our planet was a giant ball of burning rock. There was no life on Earth.

When the giant plates that form the Earth's surface moved and bumped into each other, they pushed magma up through holes, causing volcanic eruptions.

The eruptions blew out hollows and dropped debris, making impressions in the Earth that would become oceans and valleys. The lava hardened, forming mountains and islands.

Air are Life!

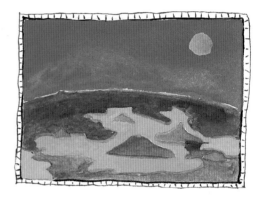

Volcanic eruptions also threw hot gas and steam into space.

The gases formed the first layers of our atmosphere, which is now the air we breathe. The steam cooled and turned into water.

The water fell to the surface of the Earth and became oceans, lakes, and rivers. Volcanoes helped create the air and water that support life on Earth.

Inside the Earth

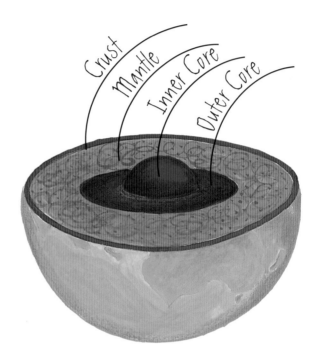

Crust
Mantle
Inner Core
Outer Core

The surface of the Earth is called the **crust**. We walk on it, and the ocean floor is also a part of it. Underneath the crust is the **mantle**. The mantle is made up of solid rock, melted rock, and hot gases. The core of the Earth is liquid on the outside and solid on the inside. The closer you are to the center of the Earth, the hotter it is!

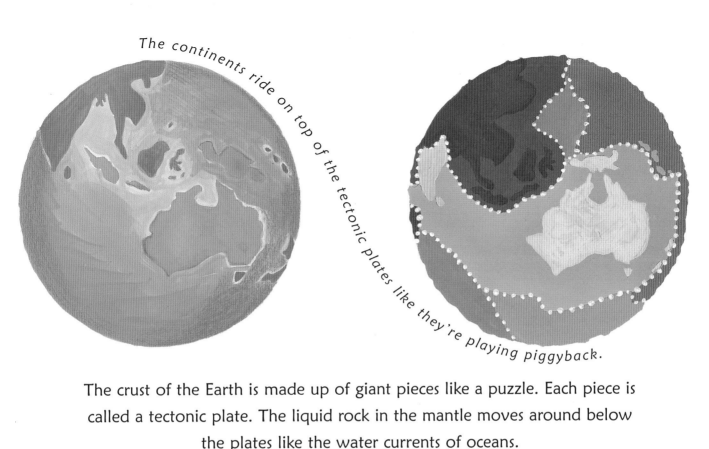

The continents ride on top of the tectonic plates like they're playing piggyback.

The crust of the Earth is made up of giant pieces like a puzzle. Each piece is called a tectonic plate. The liquid rock in the mantle moves around below the plates like the water currents of oceans.

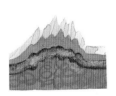  

The tectonic plates ride on top of the moving liquid rock of the mantle. The plates touch and rub together, pushing and sliding on top of each other. This creates tremendous pressure, which causes the Earth's crust to rise up. The **magma** that explodes out of volcanoes is made up of liquid rock and gas.

A Volcano

Magma is found beneath the surface of the Earth. It rises into the Earth's crust, pushed upward by gas. The magma flows up and quickly fills underground pockets and reservoirs. If the pressure continues to build, the crust is pushed up and a mountain forms. If the magma breaks through the crust, the volcano will erupt!

Is Born

When magma is trapped just below the surface of the Earth, it's still called magma. When it explodes from the volcano, it's called **lava**. When the volcano erupts, the top of the mountain is blown into the air. After the eruption, there will be a **crater** where the top used to be. Big clouds of smoke and gas rise from the top of the volcano. That's not fire— it's red-hot lava! After the lava cools, it turns gray or black.

There are more than 40,000 active volcanoes on the planet. We can't see most of them because they're on the bottom of the ocean. Most of these volcanoes are beneath the Pacific Ocean in an area called The Ring of Fire. There are about 1,000 active volcanoes on dry land around the world.

People who study volcanoes are called volcanologists. They walk right up to the craters of volcanoes to make measurements, set up observation posts, and take photos. They dress like astronauts with boots, helmets, and special heat-resistant suits to protect them from the high temperatures.

Eldfell

Helgafell

Surtsey

Mount Etna

Puy de Dome

Stromboli

ATLANTIC OCEAN

Erta Alé

INDIAN OCEAN   Kraka

Kilimanjaro

Piton De La Fournais

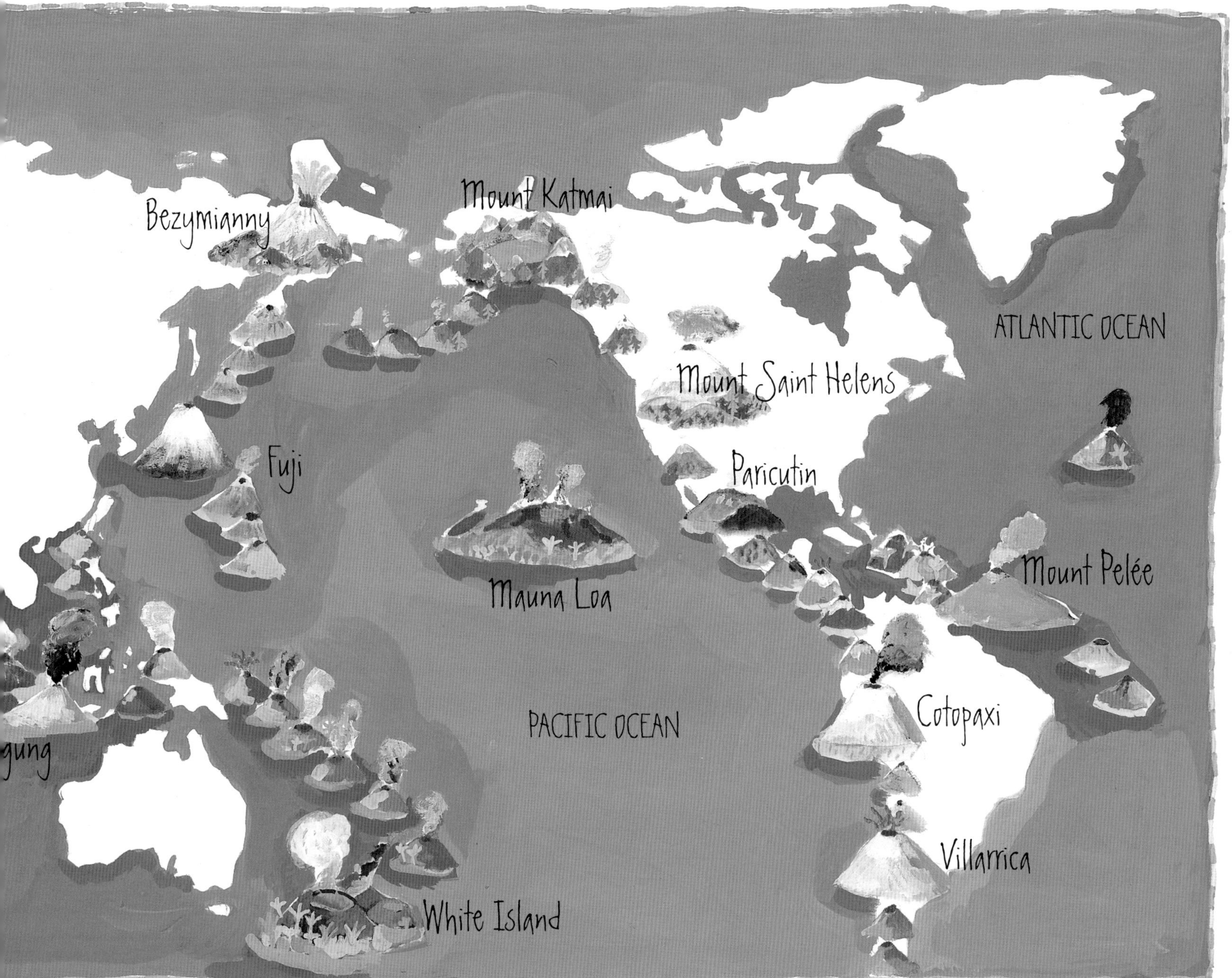

Bezymianny

Mount Katmai

ATLANTIC OCEAN

Mount Saint Helens

Paricutin

Fuji

Mauna Loa

Mount Pelée

PACIFIC OCEAN

Cotopaxi

gung

Villarrica

White Island

Volcanic Eruptions

The shape of a volcano depends on its eruptions. Some spit out runny lava that flows like a river. Others project rocky lava. Some volcanoes only release gas, smoke, steam, or ashes. Some do all of this at once. Volcanoes are grouped into families by the way they explode.

The Pelean Family

The thick lava inside these volcanoes doesn't flow very far. It builds up inside, forming a cone-shaped mountain. There's a lot of pressure—and explosive potential—trapped inside this mountain.

In 1902, **Mount Pelee** erupted. Mount Pelee is a volcano on Martinique, an island in the East Caribbean Sea. It completely destroyed the village of Saint Pierre.

The Hawaiian Family

*This family's runny lava flows for miles before it cools and stops. It slowly builds a broad, sloping cone around the volcano. The **Mauna Loa** volcano in Hawaii is the biggest volcano in the world. It begins at the bottom of the Pacific Ocean and is more than 29,527 feet tall. That's taller than Mount Everest!*

The Vulcanian Family

*In **Vulcanian** volcanoes, magma trapped beneath hardened lava builds up pressure until it explodes. Clouds of gas and dust form above the crater. The island of Sicily was made by a Vulcanian volcano.*

The Strombolian Family

*The explosions of these volcanoes are very mild, but they happen a lot. They usually send clouds of gas and ash into the air, and a little bit of runny lava comes out. This lava isn't nearly as runny as the lava of the Hawaiian volcanoes. The **Stromboli** volcano in Sicily has been continuously active for more than 2,000 years.*

An Unusual Place

There is a special place in central France called Auvergne. One hundred different kinds of volcanoes form a long chain. Some have rounded domes. Some have pointed cones. Some have craters on top. Sometimes, small craters form inside a large crater. Their sides are covered with plants.

A chapel stands on the top of an ancient volcano in Auvergne.

Volcanoes can erupt at any time, even if we think they have been extinct for millions of years. Sometimes people build houses around volcanoes they believe are extinct. When the volcano erupts, the houses are destroyed.

Volcanoes at the Bottom of the Ocean

The Earth's crust is much thinner beneath the ocean.
It's easy for a gash or slit to form on the ocean floor.
Then lava can escape. So, there are many more
volcanoes here than there are above the ground.

Some volcanoes form gigantic islands. These islands, like some in the Pacific, may be surrounded by coral. When the highest point of a volcano wears down and falls beneath the surface of the water, the coral remains. It forms a ring around the place where the top of the volcano used to be. This ring is called an **atoll**. In the center is a **lagoon**.

Underwater eruptions are spectacular. Gases, debris, and extremely hot lava hit the freezing cold water in steamy explosions. These explosions move great quantities of water, creating huge waves called **tsunamis**.

When a Volcano Erupts

These are the things you'll see during and after an eruption.

The **cloud** over a volcano is the most dangerous part of an explosion. These clouds are made of rock, ash, and hot poisonous gases.

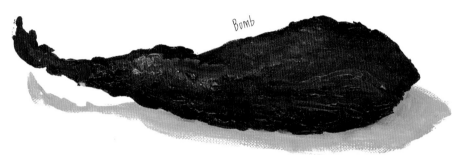

Bomb

Eruption clouds

Bombs are the biggest pieces of lava. They start out soft, get round as they fly through the air, and harden before they hit the ground.

The small drops of solid lava are called **lapilli.**

Lapilli

Sulphur

Tiny, hair-like threads of glass are made from molten basalt. This is called **Pele's hair.**

Pumice stone

Pumice stone is hardened lava. Trapped gas bubbles create lots of little hollow places in the rock, so it's very light. Pumice is the only rock that can float on water.

Volcanic ash

The **ashes** of volcanoes are actually pieces of lava the size of sand.

Pele's hair

The hot **lava** covers everything in its path. It flows until it hardens. Sometimes lava flows more than 620 miles.

Lava flow

They fly high into the sky and get carried away by the wind.

The Benefits of Volcanoes

Obsidian

Granite

Mica

In some hot and humid climates, volcanic ash **fertilizes** the soil. Volcanic ash is full of important nutrients and minerals, so plants grow well in these places. Lava usually fertilizes the soil too. It burns up nutrients as it flows out of the volcano. As the cooled lava breaks down, the nutrients return to the soil.

Basalt

If you look through a magnifying glass at a piece of cooled lava (such as **basalt**), you can see small crystals. The crystals are minerals that were melted in the magma deep inside the Earth. When the lava exploded from the volcano and cooled, the minerals formed crystals. You can see crystals in **granite** and **mica**, too, because they're volcanic rocks. Volcanic rock is very strong.

Plant growth on a piece of lava.

Gold

Volcanic mud

Gold

Geysers are jets of warm water and steam that shoot out of old volcanoes. They spurt from the ground like big fountains.

In Hawaii, New Zealand, and Iceland, people use the steam to make electricity.

People in Italy and Japan bathe in volcanic mud, which is good for your skin and fights rheumatism.

Volcanoes put important **minerals,** such as sulphur, back into the ground. They also create gold and other precious stones. In South Africa, you can find diamonds inside the ancient chimneys of volcanoes.

A rough diamond

A cut diamond

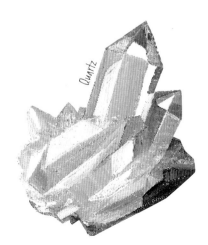
Quartz

The Legend of the Volcanoes of Auvergne

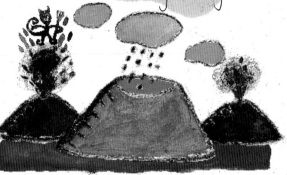

 The people of Auvergne believe that the Christian god sent all the demons to the center of the Earth. The demons could only see the sky through very small holes, so they made the holes bigger, sending up flames and smoke. God made it rain to put out the fires, filling all the holes with holy water. This is why so many of the craters at Auvergne have lakes in them.

Pele

Hawaiian Goddess of Fire

In Hawaii, the goddess Pele lives inside the Kilauea crater. She is the goddess of fire, dancing, volcanoes, and violence. The islanders hold ceremonies, pray, and make sacrifices in her honor.

In Greek mythology, the god Hephaestus had a forge beneath Mount Etna. He made armor and weapons for the gods there.

Hephaestus

& History

Vesuvius

One morning in 1943, a farmer was working in his fields in Mexico. Suddenly, the Earth started to tremble. The farmer ran to warn the villagers of Paricutin.

Paricutin

Mexico

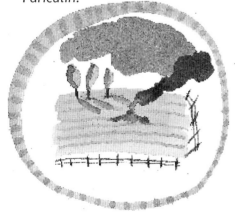

When he arrived, he found a small hill that hadn't been there before. The next day it had become an enormous volcano. Now, Paricutin is completely covered with lava—except for the bell tower of the church!

Pompeii Italy

Two ancient towns, Pompeii and Herculaneum, were built at the foot of Mount Vesuvius. In the year 79, Mount Vesuvius erupted. The people were instantly killed by the poisonous cloud that came from the volcano. Then the towns were buried in volcanic ash and mud. Centuries later, these towns were excavated by archeologists.

Now that you know all about volcanoes of the world,
you can have fun with your poster and stickers!

Arctic Ocean

Atlantic Ocean

Pacific Ocean

Indian Ocean

Put the volcano stickers on the map of the world. If you
can't remember where a volcano is, look in the book.

Make a flipbook that shows a volcanic eruption! Cut out each picture. Put them in order using the numbers on the back.

Glue them together along the left edge of the flipbook.

Stack each page directly on top of the others. The flipbook will work better if you do this very carefullly.

After the glue has dried, hold the flipbook as shown. Use your thumb to flip it.

Congratulations! You made a fantastic volcanic eruption!

Don't dance on a volcano.

—French proverb

Other books in the My Favorite Nature Book series include:

Animals in Their Homes

Animals on the Farm

Stars & Planets